MEDIKIDZ EXPLAIN DEPRESSION

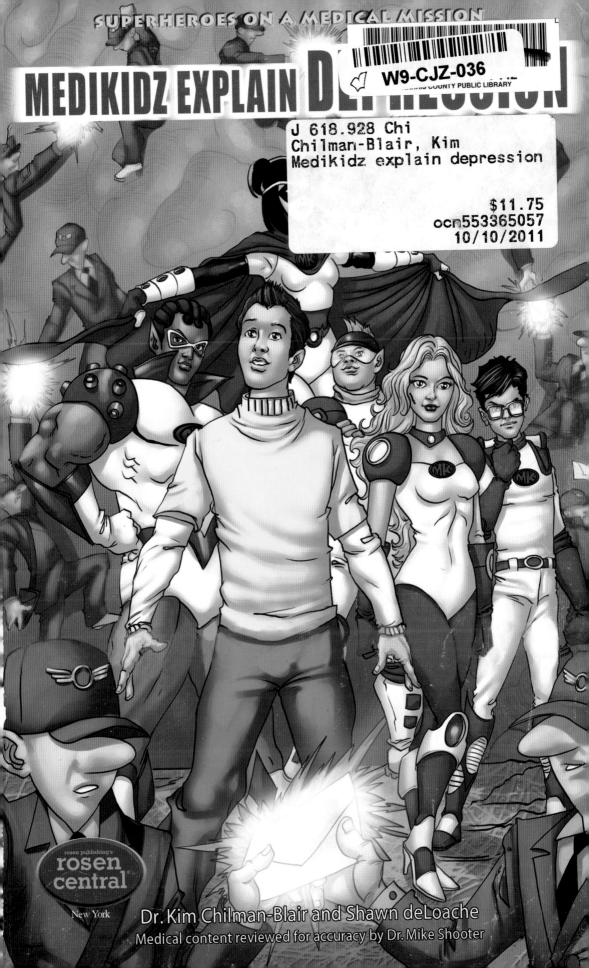

rosen publishing's
rosen central
New York

Dr. Kim Chilman-Blair and Shawn deLoache

Medical content reviewed for accuracy by Dr. Mike Shooter

This edition published in 2011 by:

The Rosen Publishing Group, Inc.
29 East 21st Street
New York, NY 10010

Additional end matter copyright © 2011 by The Rosen Publishing Group, Inc.

Library of Congress Cataloging-in-Publication Data

Chilman-Blair, Kim.
Medikidz explain depression / Kim Chilman-Blair and Shawn deLoache.
    p. cm. — (Superheroes on a medical mission)
"Medical content reviewed for accuracy by Dr. Mike Shooter."
Includes bibliographical references and index.
ISBN 978-1-4358-9455-6 (library binding) — ISBN 978-1-4488-1837-2 (pbk.)
— ISBN 978-1-4488-1838-9 (6-pack)
1. Depression in children—Comic books, strips, etc. 2. Depression, Mental—Comic books, strips, etc. I. Deloache, Shawn II. Title.
RJ506.D4C473 2011
618.92'8527—dc22

                                2010008833

Manufactured in China

CPSIA Compliance Information: Batch #MS0102YA: For further information, contact Rosen Publishing, New York, New York, at 1-800-237-9932.

JAMES! DID YOU FORGET WE HAD A DATE LAST NIGHT?

I WAITED OUTSIDE THE THEATER FOR AN HOUR!

WHAT'S WRONG WITH YOU?

I'M JUST TIRED... EXHAUSTED.

SORRY, GINA.

THAT'S IT! I'M LEAVING.

CALL ME WHEN YOU GET A CLUE.

SLAM!

JAMES SEEMS DEPRESSED...

HE DIDN'T EAT HIS BACON!

JAMES NEEDS SOMEONE TO HELP HIM UNDERSTAND HIS DEPRESSION.

TO THE MEDI-JET!

ZOOOOM

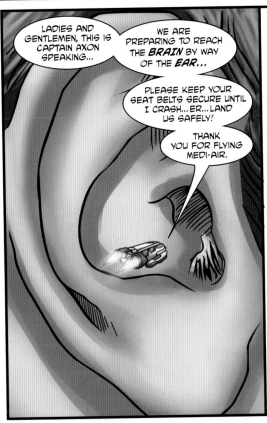

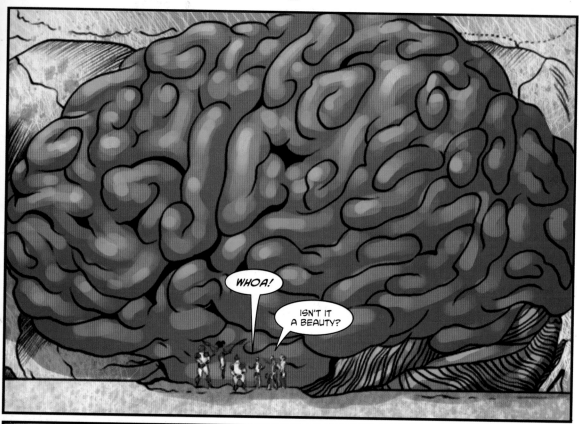

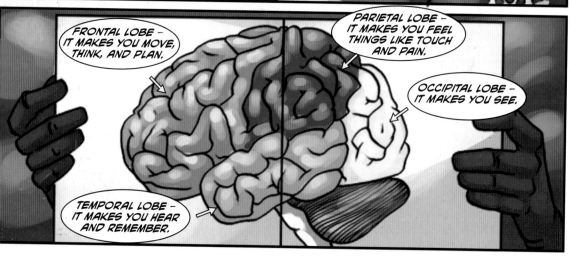

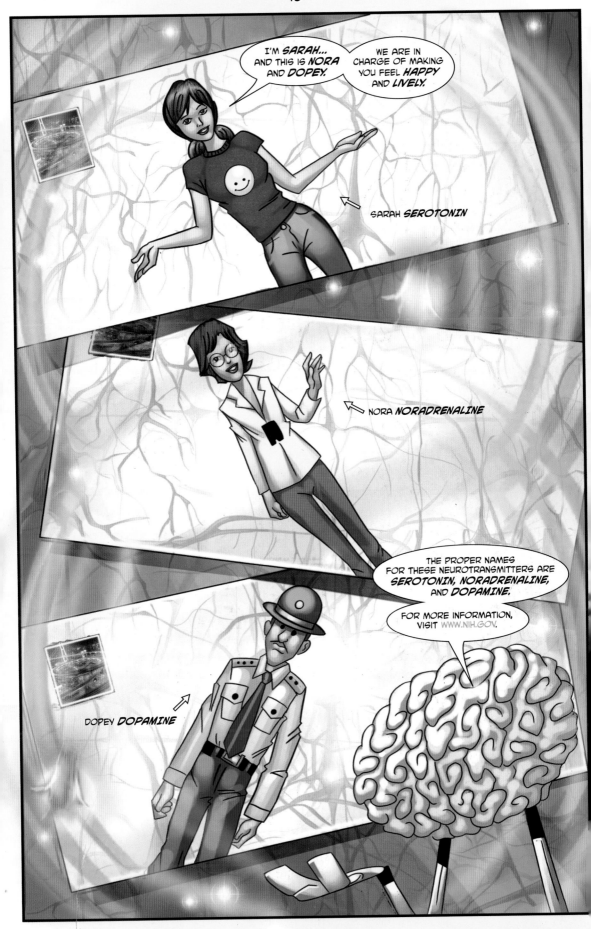

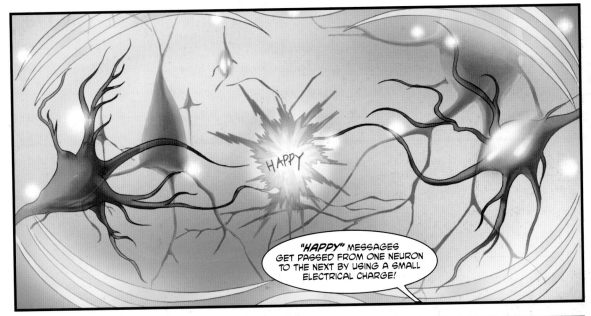

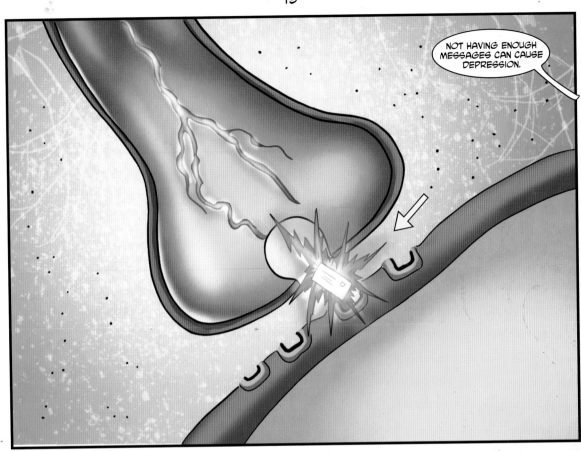

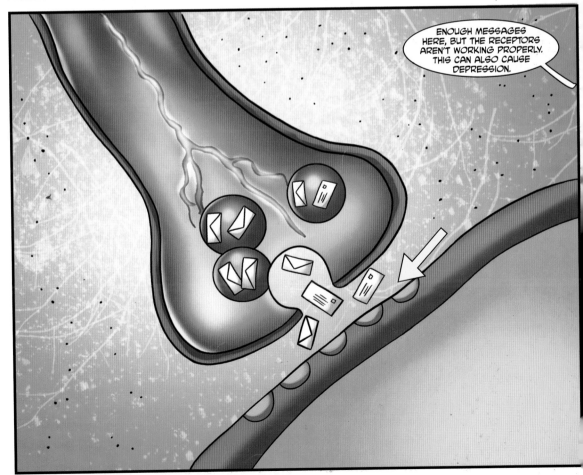

TALK THERAPY IS USUALLY THE *FIRST* THING A DOCTOR WILL SUGGEST.

YOU'LL MEET WITH A PSYCHIATRIST OR PSYCHOLOGIST.

THEY ARE BOTH EXPERTS AT HELPING PEOPLE DEAL WITH THEIR FEELINGS.

TELL ME, AXON, WHY DO YOU THINK YOU'RE SO ANGRY ALL THE TIME?

BECAUSE YOU WON'T LEAVE ME ALONE AND YOU MAKE ME ANGRY! ALSO...I WISH I WAS TALLER. OK, MY TURN. SWITCH!

HOW IS *TALKING* GOING TO HELP ME FEEL BETTER?

TALKING LETS YOU EXPRESS YOUR FEELINGS, THOUGHTS, AND BEHAVIOR...

IT'S THE FIRST STEP TO *UNDERSTANDING* THEM.

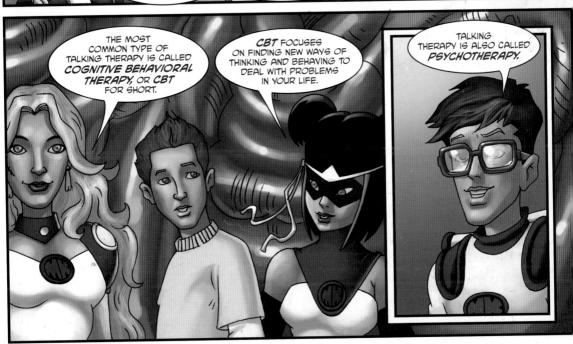

THE MOST COMMON TYPE OF TALKING THERAPY IS CALLED *COGNITIVE BEHAVIORAL THERAPY,* OR *CBT* FOR SHORT.

CBT FOCUSES ON FINDING NEW WAYS OF THINKING AND BEHAVING TO DEAL WITH PROBLEMS IN YOUR LIFE.

TALKING THERAPY IS ALSO CALLED *PSYCHOTHERAPY.*

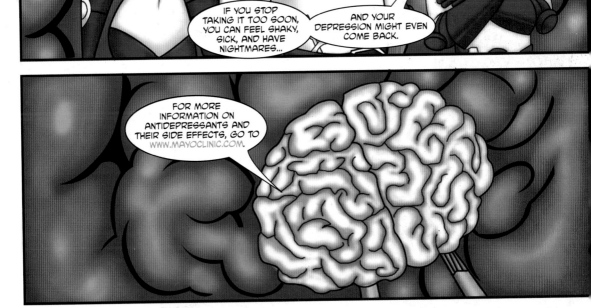

5 WEEKS LATER...

Dr.Carson
PSYCHIATRIST

WOW, DEPRESSION ISN'T AS SCARY AS I THOUGHT.

I FEEL SO MUCH BETTER ALREADY.

IT SURE IS NICE TO KNOW I CAN FEEL HAPPY AGAIN!

HI, JAMES. I'M READY FOR YOU NOW.

AND THANKS TO THE MEDIKIDZ, I'M READY, TOO.

KNOCK KNOCK

WHAT ARE YOU DOING HERE?

UMMM... THESE ARE FOR YOU.

I THOUGHT MAYBE WE COULD GO TO SEE A FILM?

OH, JAMES! YOU'RE SO SWEET!

AGITATED BEING TROUBLED OR NERVOUS.

ANTIDEPRESSANT A DRUG THAT IS PRESCRIBED BY A DOCTOR TO PREVENT OR REDUCE DEPRESSION.

BRAIN THE CENTER OF THE HUMAN NERVOUS SYSTEM. IT CONTROLS THOUGHT, INVOLUNTARY MOVEMENT IN THE BODY, BALANCE, GROWTH, AND TEMPERATURE CONTROL.

COGNITIVE BEHAVIORAL THERAPY ALSO KNOWN AS COGNITIVE THERAPY; A VERY STRUCTURED THERAPY METHOD THAT AIMS TO HELP PEOPLE IN THE WAYS THEY THINK (THE COGNITIVE) AND THE WAYS THEY ACT (THE BEHAVIOR). IT IS BASED ON THE CONCEPT THAT THE WAY PEOPLE THINK ABOUT THINGS AFFECTS THEIR EMOTIONS. THE THERAPY FOCUSES ON PRESENT THINKING, BEHAVIOR, AND COMMUNICATION INSTEAD OF PAST EXPERIENCES, AND IT IS GEARED TOWARD PROBLEM SOLVING.

DEPRESSED BEING UNHAPPY, SAD, OR FEELING HOPELESS.

DOPAMINE A CHEMICAL COMPOUND THAT OCCURS IN THE BRAIN; A NEUROTRANSMITTER.

EMOTION A STRONG FEELING ABOUT SOMEONE OR SOMETHING.

ENVIRONMENT A SET OF EXTERNAL CONDITIONS, PARTICULARLY THOSE AFFECTING A CERTAIN ACTIVITY; SURROUNDING INFLUENCES.

FRONTAL LOBE THE PART OF THE BRAIN THAT IS LOCATED AT THE FRONT OF EACH CEREBRAL HEMISPHERE. IT IS ASSOCIATED WITH REASONING, PLANNING, PARTS OF SPEECH AND MOVEMENT, EMOTIONS, AND PROBLEM SOLVING.

GENE THE BASIC UNIT OF HEREDITY, WHICH IS ABLE TO TRANSMIT CHARACTERISTICS FROM ONE GENERATION TO THE NEXT.

LIMBIC SYSTEM A GROUP OF BRAIN STRUCTURES AND THEIR CONNECTIONS, LOCATED NEAR THE BRAIN STEM, THAT IS THOUGHT TO CONTROL EMOTIONS, BEHAVIOR, AND SMELL, AMONG OTHER THINGS.

LOBES ROUNDED DIVISIONS OR PROJECTIONS OF ORGANS OR PARTS IN THE BODY, ESPECIALLY IN THE LUNGS, BRAIN, OR LIVER.

MORPH TO TRANSFORM QUICKLY.

NEURONS CELLS OF THE NERVOUS SYSTEM THAT ARE SPECIALIZED TO CARRY "MESSAGES" TO AND FROM THE BRAIN AND TO OTHER PARTS OF THE BODY.

NEUROTRANSMITTERS CHEMICAL SUBSTANCES PRODUCED BY THE BODY THAT ACT AS MESSENGERS OR SIGNAL CARRIERS.

NORADRENALINE ALSO KNOWN AS NOREPINEPHRINE; A HORMONE AND NEUROTRANSMITTER, SECRETED BY THE

ADRENAL GLAND. IT INCREASES BLOOD PRESSURE AND RATE AND DEPTH OF BREATHING, RAISES THE LEVEL OF BLOOD SUGAR, AND DECREASES THE ACTIVITY OF THE INTESTINES.

OCCIPITAL LOBE THE PYRAMID-SHAPED PART OF THE BRAIN THAT IS LOCATED AT THE BACK OF EACH HEMISPHERE. IT ACTS AS THE VISUAL PROCESSING CENTER OF THE BRAIN.

PARIETAL LOBE THE PART OF THE BRAIN THAT IS LOCATED ABOVE THE OCCIPITAL LOBE AND BEHIND THE FRONTAL LOBE. IT IS CONCERNED WITH STIMULI RELATED TO TOUCH, PRESSURE, TEMPERATURE, AND PAIN.

PSYCHIATRIST A DOCTOR WHO IS TRAINED IN THE TREATMENT OF PEOPLE WHO HAVE MENTAL DISORDERS.

PSYCHOLOGIST AN EXPERT OR SPECIALIST WHO IS TRAINED TO PERFORM RESEARCH, TESTING, AND THERAPY FOR DISORDERS OF THE BRAIN AND BEHAVIORAL PROBLEMS.

PSYCHOTHERAPY THE TREATMENT OF MENTAL DISORDERS BY PSYCHOLOGICAL METHODS.

RECEPTOR A NERVE ENDING THAT IS SENSITIVE TO STIMULI AND CAN CONVERT THEM INTO NERVE IMPULSES.

SELECTIVE SEROTONIN REUPTAKE INHIBITOR (SSRI) A DRUG THAT INCREASES SEROTONIN LEVELS IN SYNAPSES, RESULTING IN THE ELEVATION OF MOOD.

SEROTONIN A CHEMICAL THAT COMES FROM THE AMINO ACID TRYPTOPHAN AND IS WIDELY DISTRIBUTED IN TISSUES. IT ACTS AS A NEUROTRANSMITTER, CONSTRICTS BLOOD VESSELS AT INJURY SITES, AND CAN AFFECT A PERSON'S EMOTIONAL STATE.

SIDE EFFECT AN UNDESIRABLE SECONDARY EFFECT OF A DRUG OR OTHER FORM OF MEDICAL TREATMENT.

SYMPTOM A PHYSICAL OR MENTAL FEATURE THAT INDICATES A CONDITION OF A DISEASE OR OTHER DISORDER, ESPECIALLY ONE EXPERIENCED BY THE PATIENT; FOR EXAMPLE, IF A PERSON FEELS PAIN, DIZZINESS, OR ITCHING.

TALK THERAPY AN APPROACH THAT STRESSES VERBAL COMMUNICATION BETWEEN A PSYCHIATRIST OR PSYCHOLOGIST AND HIS OR HER PATIENT TO TREAT AN EMOTIONAL OR MENTAL DISORDER.

TEMPORAL LOBE THE PART OF THE BRAIN THAT IS LOCATED ON BOTH THE RIGHT AND LEFT SIDES. IT IS CONCERNED WITH HEARING AND MEMORY.

FOR MORE INFORMATION

AMERICAN ACADEMY OF CHILD AND ADOLESCENT PSYCHIATRY
3615 WISCONSIN AVENUE NW
WASHINGTON, DC 20016-3007
(202) 966-7300
WEB SITE: HTTP://WWW.AACAP.ORG
THIS NONPROFIT ORGANIZATION SUPPORTS AND ADVANCES
        CHILD AND TEEN PSYCHIATRY THROUGH RESEARCH AND
        DISTRIBUTION OF INFORMATION.

CANADIAN MENTAL HEALTH ASSOCIATION (CMHA)
PHOENIX PROFESSIONAL BUILDING
595 MONTREAL ROAD, SUITE 303
OTTAWA, ON K1K 4L2
CANADA
(613) 745-7750
WEB SITE: HTTP://WWW.CMHA.CA
THE CMHA PROVIDES PROGRAMS FOR CANADIANS WHO HAVE
        MENTAL ILLNESSES. IT PUBLISHES MATERIALS ON MENTAL
        DISORDERS, INCLUDING DEPRESSION.

DEPRESSION AND BIPOLAR SUPPORT ALLIANCE
730 NORTH FRANKLIN STREET, SUITE 501
CHICAGO, IL 60654-7225
(800) 826-3632
WEB SITE: HTTP://WWW.NDMDA.ORG
THIS PATIENT-DIRECTED ORGANIZATION PROVIDES INFORMATION
        AND EDUCATIONAL MATERIALS ABOUT DEPRESSION AND
        BIPOLAR DISORDER.

INTERNATIONAL FOUNDATION FOR RESEARCH AND EDUCATION
ON DEPRESSION (IFRED)
P.O. BOX 17598
BALTIMORE, MD 21297-1598
(410) 268-0044
WEB SITE: HTTP://WWW.IFRED.ORG
IFRED IS DEDICATED TO RESEARCHING CAUSES OF DEPRESSION
        AND SUPPORTING THOSE DEALING WITH THE CONDITION.

MENTAL HEALTH AMERICA
2000 NORTH BEAUREGARD STREET, 6TH FLOOR
ALEXANDRIA, VA 22311
(800) 969-6642
WEB SITE: HTTP://WWW.MENTALHEALTHAMERICA.NET
MENTAL HEALTH AMERICA IS THE OLDEST AND LARGEST
        ORGANIZATION IN THE UNITED STATES THAT ADDRESSES
        ALL ASPECTS OF MENTAL HEALTH AND ILLNESS.

MOOD DISORDERS SOCIETY OF CANADA
3-304 STONE ROAD WEST, SUITE 736
GUELPH, ON N1G 4W4
CANADA
(519) 824-5565
WEB SITE: HTTP://WWW.MOODDISORDERSCANADA.CA
THE MOOD DISORDERS SOCIETY OF CANADA WORKS TO
       IMPROVE THE QUALITY OF LIFE FOR PEOPLE AFFECTED BY
       DEPRESSION AND RELATED DISORDERS.

NATIONAL INSTITUTE OF MENTAL HEALTH (NIMH)
6001 EXECUTIVE BOULEVARD
ROOM 8184, MSC 9663
BETHESDA, MD 20892-9663
(866) 615-6464
WEB SITE: HTTP://WWW.NIMH.NIH.GOV
THIS FEDERAL AGENCY CONDUCTS RESEARCH ON MENTAL
       HEALTH, INCLUDING THE CAUSES, PREVENTION, DIAGNOSIS,
       AND TREATMENT OF MENTAL ILLNESSES. IT ALSO OFFERS
       PUBLICATIONS ON UNDERSTANDING AND TREATING MENTAL
       ILLNESSES.

NATIONAL MENTAL HEALTH INFORMATION CENTER
P.O. BOX 2345
ROCKVILLE, MD 20847
(800) 789-2647
WEB SITE: HTTP://MENTALHEALTH.SAMHSA.GOV
THE NATIONAL MENTAL HEALTH INFORMATION CENTER (A PART
       OF THE SUBSTANCE ABUSE AND MENTAL HEALTH SERVICES
       ADMINISTRATION) PROVIDES INFORMATION ABOUT MENTAL
       HEALTH AND DEPRESSION BY TELEPHONE, WEB SITE, AND
       THROUGH MORE THAN SIX HUNDRED PUBLICATIONS.

WEB SITES

DUE TO THE CHANGING NATURE OF INTERNET LINKS, ROSEN
PUBLISHING HAS DEVELOPED AN ONLINE LIST OF WEB SITES
RELATED TO THE SUBJECT OF THIS BOOK. THIS SITE IS UPDATED
REGULARLY. PLEASE USE THIS LINK TO ACCESS THIS LIST:

HTTP://WWW.ROSENLINKS.COM/MED/DEPR

FOR FURTHER READING

BERNAY, EMMA. *CONTEMPORARY ISSUES COMPANION.* DETROIT, MI: GREENHAVEN PRESS, 2007.

BJORNLUND, LYDIA. *DEPRESSION (DISEASES AND DISORDERS).* DETROIT, MI: LUCENT, 2010.

HIPP, EARL. *FIGHTING INVISIBLE TIGERS: A STRESS MANAGEMENT GUIDE FOR TEENS.* MINNEAPOLIS, MN: FREE SPIRIT PUBLISHING, 2008.

LANGWITH, JACQUELINE. *DEPRESSION (PERSPECTIVES ON DISEASES AND DISORDERS).* DETROIT, MI: GREENHAVEN PRESS, 2008.

LUCAS, EILEEN. *MORE THAN THE BLUES? UNDERSTANDING AND DEALING WITH DEPRESSION (ISSUES IN FOCUS TODAY).* BERKELEY HEIGHTS, NJ: ENSLOW PUBLISHERS, 2009.

KITTLESON, MARK J. *THE TRUTH ABOUT FEAR AND DEPRESSION.* NEW YORK, NY: FACTS ON FILE, 2004.

MARTIN, MICHAEL. *TEEN DEPRESSION.* DETROIT, MI: LUCENT, 2004.

MILLER, ALLEN R. *LIVING WITH DEPRESSION (TEEN'S GUIDES).* NEW YORK, NY: FACTS ON FILE, 2007.

NUNN, LAURA SILVERSTEIN, ALVIN SILVERSTEIN, AND VIRGINIA SILVERSTEIN. *THE DEPRESSION AND BIPOLAR DISORDER UPDATE (DISEASES UPDATE).* BERKELEY HEIGHTS, NJ: ENSLOW PUBLISHERS, 2008.

PETERSON, JUDY MONROE. *FREQUENTLY ASKED QUESTIONS ABOUT ANTIDEPRESSANTS (FAQ: TEEN LIFE).* NEW YORK, NY: ROSEN PUBLISHING GROUP, INC., 2010.

PIQUEMAL, MICHEL, AND MELISSA DALY. *WHEN LIFE STINKS: HOW TO DEAL WITH YOUR BAD MOODS, BLUES, AND DEPRESSION.* NEW YORK: NY: AMULET BOOKS, 2004.

THAKKAR, VATSAL. *DEPRESSION AND BIPOLAR DISORDER (PSYCHOLOGICAL DISORDERS).* NEW YORK, NY: CHELSEA HOUSE PUBLISHERS, 2006.

WILLIS, LAURA. *DEPRESSION (SOCIAL ISSUES FIRSTHAND).* DETROIT, MI: GREENHAVEN PRESS, 2007.

ZUCKER, FAYE, AND JOAN E. HUEBL. *BEATING DEPRESSION: TEENS FIND LIGHT AT THE END OF THE TUNNEL.* NEW YORK, NY: FRANKLIN WATTS, 2007.

INDEX

ABOUT THE AUTHORS

DR. KIM CHILMAN-BLAIR IS A MEDICAL DOCTOR WITH
TEN YEARS OF EXPERIENCE IN MEDICAL WRITING AND A
PASSION FOR PROVIDING MEDICAL INFORMATION THAT
MAKES CHILDREN WANT TO LEARN.

SHAWN DELOACHE HAS EARNED DEGREES IN PSYCHOLOGY
AND CRIMINAL JUSTICE FROM THE UNIVERSITY OF GEORGIA
IN ATHENS, GEORGIA. HE HAS WORKED WITH CHILDREN AS
A COUNSELOR, TEACHER, AND MARTIAL ARTS INSTRUCTOR,
AND CURRENTLY WORKS WITH SPECIAL NEEDS CHILDREN.
HE MOVED TO NEW YORK IN 2006 TO PURSUE A WRITING
CAREER IN NOVELS, TELEVISION, AND COMICS.